A Play

by

WILLY HOLTZMAN

Dramatic Publishing
Woodstock, Illinois • England • Australia • New Zealand

*** NOTICE ***

The amateur and stock acting rights to this work are controlled exclusively by THE DRAMATIC PUBLISHING COMPANY without whose permission in writing no performance of it may be given. Royalty fees are given in our current catalog and are subject to change without notice. Royalty must be paid every time a play is performed whether or not it is presented for profit and whether or not admission is charged. A play is performed any time it is acted before an audience. All inquiries concerning amateur and stock rights should be addressed to:

DRAMATIC PUBLISHING
P. O. Box 129, Woodstock, Illinois 60098

COPYRIGHT LAW GIVES THE AUTHOR OR THE AUTHOR'S AGENT THE EXCLUSIVE RIGHT TO MAKE COPIES. This law provides authors with a fair return for their creative efforts. Authors earn their living from the royalties they receive from book sales and from the performance of their work. Conscientious observance of copyright law is not only ethical, it encourages authors to continue their creative work. This work is fully protected by copyright. No alterations, deletions or substitutions may be made in the work without the prior written consent of the publisher. No part of this work may be reproduced or transmitted in any form or by any means, electronic or mechanical, including photocopy, recording, videotape, film, or any information storage and retrieval system, without permission in writing from the publisher. It may not be performed either by professionals or amateurs without payment of royalty. All rights, including but not limited to the professional, motion picture, radio, television, videotape, foreign language, tabloid, recitation, lecturing, publication and reading, are reserved.

For performance of any songs and recordings mentioned in this play which are in copyright, the permission of the copyright owners must be obtained or other songs and recordings in the public domain substituted.

©MMII by
WILLY HOLTZMAN

Printed in the United States of America
All Rights Reserved
(HEARTS)

For inquiries concerning all other rights, contact:
Joyce Ketay, The Joyce Ketay Agency,
1501 Broadway, Suite 1908, New York NY 10036
Phone: (212) 354-6825, Fax: (212) 354-6732

ISBN: 1-58342-093-2

for Don and Ev

IMPORTANT BILLING AND CREDIT REQUIREMENTS

All producers of the play *must* give credit to the author(s) of the play in all programs distributed in connection with performances of the play and in all instances in which the title of the play appears for purposes of advertising, publicizing or otherwise exploiting the play and/or a production. The name of the author(s) *must* also appear on a separate line, on which no other name appears, immediately following the title, and *must* appear in size of type not less than fifty percent the size of the title type. Biographical information on the author(s), if included in this book, may be used on all programs. *On all programs this notice must appear:*

"Produced by special arrangement with
THE DRAMATIC PUBLISHING COMPANY of Woodstock, Illinois"

It must be a shock to learn about the contours of your life from the pages of *Time* magazine. But when my father read the cover story about the 50th anniversary of D-Day, he immediately called me. "There are guys in here who suffer insomnia, mood swings, substance abuse—that's me!" Of course, his substance of choice was always food. Still, the sleeplessness, the bouts of depression, the flashbacks were all too familiar. The article even gave it a name: Posttraumatic Stress Disorder.

Naming something doesn't necessarily explain it. The truth about the "Greatest Generation" is that it has invisible wounds, terrible secrets, untold stories. And what obligation does that create for the "Me Generation"? Do we ignore those stories, or do we tell them, even if it means opening old wounds? The question had added urgency for me since I'm a playwright and playwrights are compulsive storytellers. When I asked my father's permission to write this play, he thoughtfully answered, "Absolutely not! I was like a million other guys. I don't want you glorifying what I did." But that's the point, I told him. How the ones who came back alive were told to resume their lives, raise families, live the American Dream and put the nightmares behind them; how the nightmares have come back in old age to haunt so many of them. I told him the process might even be healing, which elicited his favorite warning, "Don't bullshit a bullshitter." It takes a storyteller to know a storyteller. He thought about it some more and said, "You're going to tell it no matter what I say, aren't you?" He gave me a grudging "yes" on the condition that I keep his identity anonymous beyond the rough outline of his life. So here goes.

My father grew up in St. Louis and graduated high school in June of 1944. He saw his first combat that December in the Battle of the Bulge and remained in the front lines as a forward observer for the artillery through the end of the war. In the spring of 1945, he witnessed something so horrific that it changed his life forever. He couldn't tell me what that was because, like the worst traumas, it had become a lost memory. His attempt to recover that memory became the mission of his later life. It is the story of *Hearts*, and you won't find it in the pages of *Time*. This is not a war story, except that each member of that generation is a kind of warrior. This is not a heroic story, because true humility rejects heroism. In the end, as my own father instinctively knew, this is not just the story of one father. This is the story of every father.

And that's all I can divulge while keeping my word to maintain anonymity. There is, however, one last detail I should share. The father in the play is named "Donald Waldman." My father's name is "Donald Holtzman." Any similarity between the two is completely intentional.

Willy Holtzman

Hearts received a workshop production at the Festival of New Works (Frank Gagliano, artistic director), on June 2, 1999. Direction was by Michael Montel. Scenic design by Richard W. Lindsay Jr., lighting design by Mark Allen Berg. The stage manager was Nancy Uffner, the festival managing director was Mary Lou Chlipala. The cast was:

Donald Waldman	WILLIAM WISE
Babe	PETER RINI
Herbie	BRUCE FAULK
Ruby	TARA GREENWAY

Hearts premiered at the People's Light and Theatre Company (Abigail Adams, artistic director), on September 13, 2000. Direction was by Melia Bensussen. Scenic design by James F. Pyne Jr., costume design by Marla J. Jurglanis, lighting design by Thomas C. Hase, dramaturgy by Lee Devin. The sound designer and stage manager was Charles T. Brastow. The cast was:

Donald Waldman	WILLIAM WISE
Babe	STEPHEN NOVELLI
Herbie	MARK LAZAR
Ruby	PAUL MESHEJIAN

HEARTS

A Full-length Play
For 4 Men and 1 Woman
(Performed in multiple roles by an ensemble of actors)

CHARACTERS

DONALD WALDMAN
BABE
HERB
RUBY

PLACE: St. Louis, Missouri, and the Western European Front of World War II.

TIME: From 1944 to the present.

MUSIC NOTE: The specific music choices indicated in the script are the playwright's preference. Should you wish to use these musical pieces, you must gain permission from the music publishers. Other musical pieces of the period may be substituted.

HEARTS

PROLOGUE

(Frank Sinatra sings "I'll Be Seeing You." A large MAN in an ill-fitting army Ike jacket stands at "parade rest." A computer sits on a desk. The MAN snaps to attention.)

DONALD *(gruffly)*. Ten-hut. Staff Sergeant Donald L. Waldman, 3rd Army, 71st Infantry Light Division, 608 Field Artillery Battalion, "HQ" Battery, Forward Observer. Service in two armies and seven corps. Advanced over eight hundred combat miles from the Ardennes in the Battle of the Bulge to Linz, Austria, on the Czech border—the farthest point east of any U.S. fighting unit in the war. *(Grins.)* Thought I was Patton for a second there, didn't you? All that regular army "spit and polish" bullshit. I'll tell you about Patton—he would have made a helluva Nazi. What made him a hero? He was our Nazi. You can have Patton. I'll take Doberman. *(Bulges his stomach, juts his jaw in a comical underbite.)* Doberman. You know, the sad-sack go-fer on the old Sergeant Bilko show? "Hey-up-hah! At ease, soldier." "Okay, Sarge." My best impression. My only impression. You don't remember Doberman? Patton, you remember. The point is that somewhere between Patton and Doberman is Waldman. Come to think of it, I do a terrific impression of me. Here's me under fire for the first time in Belgium. *(Cowering, abject terror.)* Here's me crossing the Rhine. *(Daintily tiptoes.)* Here's me if the war went on another six months. *(Prone, dead.)* No joking matter? Go where I've gone, see what I've seen—joking's about the only thing that still makes sense. This is the Ike jacket I wore the day I came home. Hail the conquering hero! *(Tries to button the jacket over his stomach.)* Inhale. *(It's no use. He exhales.)* Forget it. So why'd I pull the damn thing out of mothballs in the first place? Here's why. *(He presses a button on the computer. The message is projected on a large screen.)* "You are cordially invited to a reunion of the 71st Infantry Division." Now there's a great idea. Let's have a bunch of old men with aluminum walkers get together and trade war stories. "The Greatest Generation Goes Senile." You want war stories? How about a chronic weight problem, which goes very nicely with my blood pressure problem, which wouldn't be caught dead without my heart problem? You think I'm afraid of dying? There are worse things, believe me. Like outliving your secrets. That's the real war story. The big secret. That you put on a uniform and killed people. I killed innocent people. And dressing up like some fucking overgrown Boy Scout won't make it go away. *(He peels off the jacket and throws it down.)* I should've thrown the damn thing out years ago.

Hearts #1 (1950)

(DONALD sits down to cards with three MEN. One of them plays in his boxer shorts.)

BABE. Is the fashion show over?

DONALD. Ev is sending a pile of clothes to Goodwill.

BABE. You're not getting rid of your parade jacket?

DONALD. I'm not planning to re-enlist. It's nothing. Rags. *(To HERBIE.)* Speaking of which, would it kill you to wear a different pair of shorts occasionally?

HERBIE. Th-these are g-good luck.

RUBY. I've got a lucky horseshoe, but I don't wear it places!

HERBIE. W-we're in a b-basement.

DONALD/BABE/RUBY. Rathskeller!

DONALD. Not that you helped nail up a single piece of paneling.

HERBIE. I was m-mowing the l-lawn.

BABE. Whose idea was "lawns," anyway?

DONALD. Probably the same guy who came up with mortgages.

RUBY. And in-laws.

BABE. And three a.m. feedings.

HERBIE. And r-rathskellers!

RUBY. Any chance we might play some hearts here?

DONALD. Okay, okay. Diamonds were led? Whose jack?

HERBIE. N-n-n-no table talk.

DONALD. No t-t-table stutter.

HERBIE. F-f-fuck you.

DONALD. Second lead of diamonds, I'm trying to determine...

RUBY. You gonna play a card, or what?

DONALD. Okay, okay—king. *(HERBIE plays the queen.)* Queen? Damn snake.

BABE. Tough break.

DONALD. Tough break, my ass. How can he drop the queen on the second lead of diamonds?

HERBIE. Like so.

DONALD. You asshole. You reneged.

HERBIE. H-h-hell I did.

BABE. I'm pretty sure he followed suit.

DONALD. Somebody reneged. Let me see the first lead.

RUBY. No looking at dead tricks.

DONALD. Who's looking? I'm investigating. *(Turns over the cards.)* There, first lead of diamonds—three diamonds and a club. You dropped a club.

HERBIE. Th-there's some rule against that?

DONALD. You don't drop points, I think you're shooting. You're shooting me in the head, is what.

RUBY. How about you play your cards, we play ours?

DONALD. Cards is exactly what I'm trying to play. So maybe you can explain why on Babe you hold off the queen of spades when on me, it's right between the eyes?

HERBIE. I d-d-don't have to explain myself.

BABE. You stopped him from shooting the moon. You're the hero.

DONALD. Better a live coward than a dead hero.

RUBY. It's just cards. Don't personalize it.

DONALD. I don't personalize it. If I personalized it I'd fucking kill him!

RUBY. Here we go again. Can we once just finish one game of hearts?

DONALD. I'm finishing. Does anyone see me not finishing?

HERBIE. I'm g-g-going.

DONALD. Who's not finishing now? Let's play.

HERBIE. "Play" means f-fun, f-frolic.

DONALD. You wanna frolic? Go frolic till your putz falls off. We'll play three-handed.

RUBY. Three-handed is not even hearts.

DONALD. It's in Hoyle. Look it up!

RUBY. So is Old Maid. And I don't play that either.

BABE. It's late. Let's call it a game.

DONALD *(to the audience)*. God, I love a good game of cards. Just you, fortune, and friends. Heaven. Unless your friends happen to be a bunch of conniving, back-stabbing, queen-dropping cocksuckers.

Let me make proper introductions: that's Herbie, the one with the slight speech impediment, only plays cards in his boxers. As you can see, that is not a boxer's physique. Since the war, he's in the junker business with his brother, Saul.

HERBIE. Ut-tility Auto P-parts, t-turn right under the G-grand Avenue viaduct.

DONALD. Ruby's the wiseguy over there, operates a pawnshop down on Hodiamont in the North End. Short a little cash before the end of the month?

RUBY. No problem. I'll fix you up four-bits on the dollar collateral. Burn the ticket, I keep your stuff. You don't like it, go get a better deal someplace else. You got merchandise to move, I move it, no questions asked.

DONALD. Call him a fence, he doesn't flinch. Call him a blood-sucking little kike, you'll be picking your teeth up off the sidewalk. Number one...

RUBY. Nobody talks to me that way!

DONALD. Number two...

RUBY. I was christened Mario Minessi at Our Lady of Sorrows Roman Catholic Church, which I attend religiously every Sunday.

DONALD. One other piece of advice—don't ever call him "wop." He'll laugh. We'll wipe the sidewalk with you, every last one of us. Except maybe Babe. Babe is like a brother to me. He's also 145 pounds soaking wet holding a bowling ball. So we're more alike in spirit than body. Not that this was always my body, but more about that later. What Babe's got is heart. Like anytime the rest of us got into a fight, he's right in there with us. Never landed a punch that I saw. Caught quite a few.

BABE. Yeah, but I never lost a fight.

DONALD. How do you win when you lose, Babe?

BABE. You show heart.

DONALD. The game breaks up like it always does because Herbie's shtupping some cocktail waitress and cards is his ticket out of the house. Guess he doesn't stutter in the sack. Ruby makes it an early night and Babe helps me clean up. We're in the basement...

DONALD/BABE. "Rathskeller."

DONALD. ...of my two bedroom ranch on Acorn Lane in Oak Estates. I'm at the window with Babe looking up and down the street.

Stein, Levene, Wolfsfeld, Schwartz...

BABE. No: Stein, Levene, Wolfsfeld, Kelly.

DONALD. Kelly? How'd he get in there?

BABE. This isn't the old neighborhood, even if half of 'em were our neighbors.

DONALD. This is not a "neighborhood." This is a development. I've got a two bedroom with a carport for a mortgage I can almost afford. This is the American Dream, Babe!

BABE. If this is the American Dream, I'm going back to sleep. You have any trouble that way?

DONALD. Dreaming?

BABE. Sleeping.

DONALD. You kidding? Before my head even hits the pillow. Of course, I wake up three or four times every night—hungry. You?

BABE. First few years out of the service, I imagined I was sleeping pretty good.

DONALD. What does imagination have to do with it? You're sleeping or you're not. *(He devours a bowl of candy)*

BABE. Hey, I don't have to tell you, one night in a foxhole your definition of sleep changes. Even after the shooting stops, the thinness of it all, the wakefulness... Now, with the new baby and all, I've become aware, I'm reminded of things not so long departed, memory things, Donnie. Things I meant to cast out, banish. Still there. The baby cries in the middle of the night, I'm already awake. The baby smiles, I cry. Some wires got crossed. Some gears, pedals. The brake is the gas, the gas is the clutch. It's hard to get from place to place in my mind, sometimes.

DONALD. It's in the past. Why're you tying yourself in knots? Life is good. We live in a clean, safe place. We're making healthy babies. We have houses, carports, rathskellers. This is what we fought for.

BABE. So why is this happening? I can't sleep like a normal person. You can't eat like a normal person.

DONALD. What are you talking about "eat"?

BABE. The way you put food into your body. It's not even eating. It's force-feeding. You barely chew. Your nose whistles. Do you even taste it?

DONALD. This is how I eat! You don't like it, fuck you.

BABE. Hey, I know you since you drank your meals out of a bottle. It was never like this!

DONALD. You got something to say, Babe? Say it!

BABE. I can't sleep! Not one night's sleep. I count sheep. Take a hot bath. Nothing works. I read an article somewhere about a cure for insomnia. I think it has possibilities. Dancing.

DONALD. Dancing makes you sleep?

BABE. Not yet. I'm hopeful. Nancy signed us up for some lessons where they paint feet on the floor. I'm starting to get it. But when I'm thinking too hard about the steps, I'm thinking too hard to sleep. Someday I won't have to think at all, and I'll be Fred Astaire. Then, how far off can sleep be? *(He assumes dance position.)* They keep telling me it's in the hips. One-two, one-two-three, one-two, one-two-three...it's not so hard.

DONALD. What do you call that?

BABE. Mambo. Cha-cha. One or the other, I forget which. You could do it.

DONALD. I don't see no taxi dancers.

BABE. With me.

DONALD. Get the fuck outta here.

BABE. We used to pee in the same toilet at the same time.

DONALD. If I knew then what I know now...

BABE. Hey, I start to date guys, I'm gonna find a better-looking guy than you. Okay, it was a stupid idea. *(BABE moves to the door.)*

DONALD. Come on. Just 'cause I said get the fuck outta here doesn't mean you gotta get the fuck outta here.
BABE. I'm tired, Donnie.
DONALD. I'm hungry. In the hips, you say? *(Beat.)* Let's dance.

(Perez Prado mambo.)

BABE. Nothing to it. One-two, one-two-three, one-two, one-two-three...
DONALD. Stop counting, for Christ's sake.
BABE *(whispers)*. One-two, one-two-three, one-two, one-two-three...
DONALD. One-two, one-two-three, one-two, one-two-three... Hey, I think I'm getting the hang of this... *(He dances within reach of the candy and empties the rest into his mouth. He is about to toss out the Ike jacket, thinks better of it and keeps it.)*

Graduation (June 1944)

DONALD & THE GUYS.
Izzie, Abie, Ikie, Sam
We're the boys that don't eat ham.
We got moxie, we got class,
If you don't like it kiss our
S-S-S-O-L, D-D-D-A-N,
Soldan, Soldan, Soldan!

DONALD. Soldan High School class of '44, the four of us—Donnie, Ruby, Herbie, Babe—smart? I don't know. Smart-ass? Natch. It was the Jewish school back then.

They say Tennessee Williams went there back before that.

BABE. No shit, went right there.

RUBY. He went when we were there, we'd've dogged him for being a cookie.

HERBIE. All wr-wr-writers are c-cookies.

DONALD. On graduation day, my dad hugs me and tells me...

DADDY. You're the first Waldman to graduate high school!

DONALD. On graduation day, my mother cries because...

MOMMA. You're not my little boychik anymore. Why didn't you finish your eggs this morning, Donell, I didn't make them the way you like? I'll make them again.

DONALD. On graduation day, I get a headline in the St. Louis Post-Dispatch...

PROJECTION: **D-day Invasion of Normandy Success. Ike Predicts War Over by Christmas.**

DONALD. On graduation day, I get a dry hump from my girlfriend in the back seat of my dad's Oldsmobile, but that's as far as she'll go, being that...

JEWISH GIRLFRIEND. I'm a NICE JEWISH GIRL!

DONALD. On graduation day, me and Babe go looking for some not-so-nice shiksas to shed our embarrassing virginity, "What's knittin', kitten?"

BABE. Hi, sugar—you rationed?

DONALD. On graduation day I get a diploma and an induction letter from the U.S. Army. I can already see my headlines: "Donald Waldman—War Hero!" Bring on the Nazis!

(Close-order drill.)

ALL. To your left, your left, your left right left...

SGT. REINECK. Private Waldman, what is the manual of arms?

DONALD. ...your left, your left...

SGT. REINECK. Private Waldman, how many fighting men in a battalion?

DONALD. ...your left right left...

SGT. REINECK. Private Waldman, what are the chances that you will ever amount to anything more than target practice for German gunners?!

DONALD. Pretty damn good, Sergeant Reineck.

I'm a "street" kid. But a Jewish street kid has a home. And that home has a bathroom. And that bathroom has a door. And if I know one thing, it's that I don't know how to take a crap in a barracks latrine with 100 other men showering, shaving, scratching their nuts and taking craps!

It's gotta be three in the morning. Hours past taps. I tiptoe back to the latrine, you'd think I was approaching an enemy sentry. I push open the door and there it is—all that tile and porcelain gleaming like a palace. All mine. Ordinarily, I'm not one to linger over body functions. But I just want it to go on and on, like a good book. I don't dare flush. Wouldn't want to wake up Sergeant Redneck. I turn to leave and he's there, BVDs like they just came back pressed from the cleaner's.

SGT. REINECK. Flush it!

DONALD. I reach for the handle.
SGT. REINECK. Look at it first. Did you hear me, Waldman?
DONALD. Yes sir.

I lean over the toilet.

SGT. REINECK. Don't you ever "sir" a sergeant! Now what do you see?
DONALD. We had chipped beef and lima beans at mess. See, hell. I'm about to pass out.
SGT. REINECK. I asked you a question. What do you see?
DONALD. Shit.
SGT. REINECK. I can't hear you!
DONALD. Shit!
SGT. REINECK. "Shit" what?
DONALD. Shit, Sergeant.
SGT. REINECK. Don't you ever shit in my latrine without my permission. Don't you eat, piss, jerk off, breathe or dream about your precious mother without my permission. You got that, Jewboy?
DONALD. Yes, Sergeant!
SGT. REINECK. Now flush!
DONALD. Whoosh! Basic training. Total military preparedness. The fine-tuned American fighting machine knows how to empty his lower tracks on orders only. Permission to pee, Sergeant. Permission to shit, Sergeant. Permission to wipe my ass, Sergeant. Permission to bleed myself dry on the battlefield, Sergeant. One last thing—you ever call me "Jewboy" when the shit is really flying, I will blow your fucking head off, Sergeant!

At Waldman Furniture, Clothing and Appliance
Friday Is Delivery Day (1952)

DONALD. I'll get back to the war in a minute. For those of you who don't know how it turned out, we won. And I lived. Problem is after you've been to war, you kinda lose your knack for living. When I got back, I couldn't see past next week, until I met a girl jitterbugged me across the dance floor at Tune Town.

(EV enters. They dance.)

EV. What's your name?
DONALD. Donnie. Don.
EV. I don't think I've seen you here, before.
DONALD. I'm not much of a fast dancer.
EV. Those are the ones to watch out for. Those are the slow dancers!

("Moonlight Serenade." DONALD dances slow and very close.)

Uhuh. Just as I thought. My name's Evelyn, in case you're interested.

DONALD. I'm interested in the National League standings. I'm interested in the price of chili dogs at O.T. Hodges. In you, I'm a lot more than interested.
EV. This is a slow dance, remember? Not so fast, sailor.
DONALD. Soldier.
EV. Okay, soldier, what did you do in the war?
DONALD. I don't like to talk about it.

EV. What are you doing since?

DONALD. I'm considering a number of career options.

EV. And what's one reason I should even give you the time of day?

DONALD. Because the war taught me I would lay down my life for love. Plus, I'm a helluva slow dancer!

(EV steps back, looks him straight in the eye, then draws close to dance. The music fades, she exits.)

She looked through me with dark soulful eyes that would maybe know what I could never say. Evelyn. Evvie. Ev. Even at the altar she looked at me that way. And in the maternity ward when she held our gorgeous little girl who had, I swear, her eyes.

(DADDY puts a pint of whiskey in front of DONALD.)

DADDY. Donnie, my boy, you're a man of responsibility, now. I know, because I'm a man of responsibility, and I'm slowing down.

DONALD. Slowing down? You threw me in the air like I was still a kid when I came back from overseas.

DADDY. I need a partner. Whattaya say? Deal?

DONALD. The last thing you need is a partner.

DADDY. Let's talk about what your baby girl needs.

DONALD. Pretty cute, huh?

DADDY. Cute? My granddaughter is beautiful. And smart!

DONALD. She's two hours old.

DADDY. You got to plan ahead. You think college is cheap?

DONALD. She's got her mother's eyes.

DADDY. And her father's heart. You know inside this is the right thing to do. Okay, it's not the high-rent district. It's not Macy's. But Ruby's pawnshop is ten blocks west on Hodiamont. Herbie's junkyard is across Grand. Babe's Army Navy is just up the street on Taylor. It's like home. Fifty-fifty, down the middle. That's my last offer. Deal?

DONALD. Deal, partner. *(They drink.)*

Welcome to the furniture business. Turns out I really don't hate the work. But what I love is Fridays. Not because it's payday for me. Because it's delivery day. I love deliveries. Especially on the fourteen hundred block of Hodiamont. I make sure that's my last call. Because roundabout five on Friday, Lowell Farely hauls Bessie's washtub off the back porch, fills it full of hickory scraps, and fans the flames with yesterday's racing results from Cahokia Downs. If the ponies were running right on Thursday, you're looking at a full rack of prime Ozark baby back...

(He holds up a slab of ribs wrapped in newspaper. HERBIE enters with BABE.)

HERBIE. Do I smell r-ribs.
DONALD. No. You do not smell my ribs.
BABE. Friends are supposed to share.
DONALD. I can always get more friends. As for schnorers who just happen to show up on rib day...
HERBIE. R-ruby called.
BABE. He said to meet here.
DONALD. He didn't say anything to me.

(RUBY enters.)

RUBY. Do I smell ribs?

DONALD. I'm not sharin' my fuckin' ribs!

RUBY. No? Not even with a guy who's got four seats right behind the Cardinals' dugout? *(RUBY fans open baseball tickets.)*

BABE. Get outta here. Box seats!

RUBY. You think I take bleacher tickets for collateral? If we hurry we can get there for batting practice.

DONALD. You go ahead. I'll catch up later.

HERBIE. If you f-feel that strongly about the ribs...

DONALD. It's not the ribs. It's business.

RUBY. What business? I bet it's four hours since the last customer walked through the door.

DONALD. Do I tell you how to run your business? Anyway, it's more of a personal matter.

RUBY. Fuck you, I'll get Stanley Spiegelman.

BABE. What's the matter, Donnie, you and Ev have a fight? Leave it to Babe. I'll give her a call and...

DONALD. Don't you say a word. She thinks we're playing cards.

HERBIE. He's f-fucking somebody.

DONALD. I am not fucking somebody. *(They don't budge an inch.)* Okay, okay. I come back from deliveries today, this guy is waiting for me in the alley. He tells me I don't make deliveries anymore. The Teamsters make deliveries for me.

HERBIE. W-what's he look like?

DONALD. Couple heads taller than me. Gold tooth. One eye kind of milky.

RUBY. You told him "yeah," right?

DONALD. I put him up against the wall and told him if he ever showed his ugly face around here again I'd kick his nuts up his nose.
RUBY. Do you have a fuckin' brain in your head? That was Frank Olivastro.
BABE. Maybe you can call somebody, Ruby.
RUBY. I know a guy down at the union hall.
DONALD. Fuck the Teamsters. And fuck Frank Olivastro. The sonofabitch spit in my face.
HERBIE. H-he'll come back. W-with friends.
DONALD. You see me going anywhere? *(He pulls a Luger and chambers a bullet.)*
BABE. Where'd you get that?
DONALD. Off an SS captain. He spit in my face, too. *(He removes the ribs from the newspaper.)*
RUBY. What's everybody getting all excited about? We'll go to the ballpark and swing by here on the way back. Anything suspicious, we call the cops.
DONALD. Enjoy the game. This isn't your problem.

(BABE and HERBIE hesitate.)

BABE. You know, those ballpark hot dogs give me gas like you wouldn't believe.
HERBIE. S-sitting that close, you can g-get hit by a foul ball.

(BABE and HERBIE pull up chairs. DONALD turns on a small table radio.)

RUBY. Are you guys completely nuts? We're talkin' box seats. The Chicago Cubs. We hate the fuckin' Cubs!

(A car engine approaches. Bright headlights glare through the window. DONALD stands defiantly with his Luger. One by one the others join him shoulder to shoulder. Hand inches toward the Luger. The engine revs. BABE reaches into his pocket and removes a hand grenade. He pulls the pin. The car races away. BABE releases the handle and they recoil. A small flame appears on the grenade.)

BABE. Cigarette lighter. Can't keep 'em in stock.

(They think that's the funniest thing they ever heard. They only stop laughing long enough to devour the ribs. An announcer's voice crackles over the radio.)

ANNOUNCER *(on radio)*. You're tuned to KMOX, the voice of the St. Louis Cardinals. And it's a beautiful night for baseball...

Winter Camping (December 1944)

(Foghorns. DONALD sways, shipboard, seasick.)

DONALD. Twenty-four days on the U.S.S. Monticello. Damn the torpedoes—the boat ride alone could kill you. Twenty-four days in the North Atlantic far from landlocked, never-swam-a-stroke-in-your-life Missouri. Twenty-four days zigging and zagging at three-quarters speed to avoid U-boats. You wonder why they issue helmets before the crossing. *This* is why!

(He's about to be sick when he hears surf on shore. Motorized equipment. Whistles. DONALD kisses the blessed shore.)

We put ashore in Le Havre as peacefully as when we left New York Harbor. They pack us off inland to the "reception" depot where non-coms check us in and call roll so often you hear the names in your sleep.

CORPORAL. Wade, Waggoner, Wailey, Waldman ... report to the stockage depot.

DONALD. ... where we get a lecture on ...

SERGEANT. Hygiene. There are two ways to get yourself killed "evacuating" your bowels in the field of battle. The first is dropping a load too near the enemy line, in which case a German sniper will just love to get your fat ass in the cross-hairs. The second is to drop a load too near your own line, in which case I will personally shoot you for leaving me downwind of that stench. Of course, the first incoming 88'll evacuate ya in a hurry no matter where you are, so bring a change of diapers. As far as body lice, frostbite, gangrene and syphilis goes ...

DONALD. Syphilis! Now you're talking. I no sooner picture willing mademoiselles than the quartermaster is issuing arms.

QUARTERMASTER. Wade, Waggoner, Wailey, Waldman ...

DONALD. I was pretty good on the range at Basic with the M-1. Killing distance up to one mile, which is the closest I ever intend to be to members of the Wehrmacht. But some corporal is shoving a carbine at me ...

QUARTERMASTER. This weapon is light, easy to carry, with a maximum effective range of .27 mile.

DONALD. Give me one of those long guns.

QUARTERMASTER. What for? FO's are usually spittin' distance from the Krauts most of the time.

DONALD. He's a country boy. Something about the military, within six months everybody is a country boy. What the hell is spitting distance? What the hell is an FO?

QUARTERMASTER. Move it, soldier.

DONALD. Brrr. When do I get my winter uniform? I know Ike was optimistic about the war being over before Christmas. But I'm headed to Belgium in the dead of winter and I'm wearing the army's answer to the seersucker suit.

SOLDIER. Pssst. Hey, brother. They give us these lightweight uniforms 'cause they don't expect us to live long enough to catch cold.

DONALD. Says who?

ANOTHER SOLDIER. Hey, buddy, what weight uniforms you think they got in the Pacific? That's where we're headed next.

DONALD. No more boats!

STILL ANOTHER SOLDIER. Nah, I got the real dope. A friend in the signal corps says we're in deep shit. 300,000 Germans split the 1st, 9th and 3rd armies and are halfway to Antwerp. They're callin' it the "Bulge."

DONALD. "Bulge"?

(Whistles blow.)

SERGEANT. Wade, Waggoner, Wailey, Waldman. Report to the 3rd Replacement Depot at once.

DONALD. Next to last stop. Repple Depple. No more guessing games. Now you can hear it, the constant shelling. Eighty-eights thrumming, distant, like thunder. No one has to tell you that the next stop might be your last. Because Ike got caught with his pants down and battalion keeps coming back for replacements to the corps.

Daybreak. Whistles blow, NCOs bark. The canvas-topped deuce-and-a-halfs rumble up like a big green funeral procession.

NCO. Wade, Waggoner, Wailey... this one's full, soldier. Next truck.
DONALD. Two hours later, the convoy scatters to random drop points. Our driver pulls up short like a New York City hack.
DRIVER. This is as far as I go. Don't wanna get stuck in the craters.
DONALD. Our deuce-and-a-half turns a tight radius and takes off fast enough to kick snow at us. Bad sign, leaving that fast. We look around and see no craters. For the briefest moment, the shelling stops. You can hear the wind in the pines. Then...

(The SHRIEKS and WHOMPS of a full-scale barrage.)

CAPTAIN. Incoming!
DONALD. A troop truck takes a direct hit. Wade, Waggoner, Wailey. Short war. And I'm running, zig-zagging. Why or where, I don't know. Like those German gunners are aiming at ME and they can't hit a moving target.
SERGEANT. Get in a fucking hole!

(DONALD dives for cover. A GI pops up. He's "MIKE.")

MIKE. Get the hell off me.
DONALD. Sorry. I'm new here.
MIKE. Hope you got a rabbit's foot.
DONALD. What?
MIKE. RABBIT'S FOOT. A FUCKING GOOD-LUCK CHARM!
DONALD. What are you talking about?
MIKE. The last three guys got into this hole with me died.
DONALD. You're saying one guy in this hole always dies?
MIKE. That's how it's been.
DONALD. You better get the fuck out, because it ain't gonna be me. I'm not dying!

(The shelling becomes deafening.)

Hearts #2—The Art of Over-Eating (1967)

(DONALD carries a tray of hors d'oeuvres and pauses in front of a television.)

LYNDON JOHNSON'S VOICE. I have asked the commanding general, General Westmoreland, what more he needs to meet this mounting aggression. He has told me. And we will meet his needs. We cannot be defeated by force of arms. We will stand in Vietnam.

(DONALD compulsively eats from the tray. EV enters.)

EV. Thirty-six. I put thirty-six pigs-in-a-blanket on that tray.

(DONALD guiltily returns them to the tray. She turns off the television.)

DONALD. It never stops.

EV. What, eating?

DONALD. I was just straightening out a few things. I don't even like pigs-in-a-blanket.

EV. You don't like Snickers bars either, but there's wrappers all over the house.

DONALD. The kids love Snickers.

EV. Blame them. I just want everything to be right for the guests.

DONALD. Four couples playing hearts and mah-jongg are not "guests."

EV. Well, Mindy is wearing the new hot-pink ranch mink Ruby bought her.

DONALD. Ruby does not buy things. He conveys them. A hot-pink hot mink.

EV. That's not the point. The point is Bernice didn't want a mink, so Herbie joined the new country club instead.

DONALD. They invented country clubs to keep out people like Herbie. Who's Herbie going to keep out?

EV. You're not listening to me. A club, a fur. It's nice to have nice things.

DONALD. We've got a son graduating high school. It would be nice to be able to pay for college so he doesn't get drafted like I did. What more do you want from me? I'm already working nights and weekends.

EV. I could go back to work.

DONALD. No wife of mine is going to work.

EV. I worked before we were married. Marriage is not a debilitating disease.

DONALD. Spending is a disease. You think spending makes people better than us? You think I want people saying I can't support my own family?

EV. Why are you turning this into some kind of personal attack? I'm only trying to help.

DONALD. I'll let you know when I need help. Anything else?

EV. Yes. Don't ruin this dinner party with your eating. *(Exits.)*

DONALD. That makes perfect sense. *(He plucks food from the tray.)*

EV *(offstage)*. Put it back. Thirty-six! Don't make me come in there and count.

(DONALD eats one, then breaks another in half making it look like two.)

DONALD. Thirty-six. Count? Don't make me laugh. Does she think she's playing with kids here? An amateur overeater could starve to death at one of her dinner parties. Here's a survival manual from a seasoned professional.

Start with the real hors d'oeuvres. This consists of eating before eating. For instance, dinner's at eight with cocktails at six, so you swing by White Castle around four-thirty. Why White Castle? They're bite-sized, meaning there's no need to bite them at all. Just swallow. And you can "buy 'em by the sack," which should just about get you to cocktails and hors d'oeuvres. When it comes to cheese, use all available gripping surfaces, and that includes the lips. It goes something like this—cut with the right hand, transfer to the left, and then up to the mouth. As the lips grip and propel the cheese through the teeth, the right hand is already cutting and the process begins all over. Just find your rhythm, like a juggler, and you can go on indefinitely. Or at least till a one-pound block of cheddar is reduced to an orange smudge on the serving dish.

That brings us to dinner, where pacing is everything. Work fast. Hold chewing to a minimum. Tasting is for sissies.

Finally, when you think dessert, think "even up." "Oh no! Someone left a jagged edge on that banana cream pie. I'll just even that up." Take care to leave another jagged edge, then even it up. This technique can carry you through vast portions of baked goods. Where's that German Chocolate cake? *(He licks his fingers and turns to the hearts' table.)*

HERBIE. W-we gonna eat or p-play hearts?
RUBY. It's one and the same for Waldman. He's been eating the queen for years.
DONALD. Did somebody make a joke?
BABE. You got icing on the cards, Donnie.
DONALD. Excuse me ladies, I didn't realize I wandered into the mah-jongg game.
HERBIE. J-just play a card.
DONALD. Okay, let's try a little arson.
RUBY. What's that supposed to mean?
DONALD. We're playing hearts. What does it always mean when we're playing hearts?
RUBY. Can you answer a simple question?
DONALD. I answered the fucking question.
RUBY. With a question.
DONALD. "Smoke" refers to leading spades in order to maybe make you eat the queen for a change, which I've

been doing on a regular basis for close to twenty years... is the answer to the fucking question.

RUBY. You didn't say "smoke." You said "arson."

DONALD. I was being colorful. I can't fucking believe what I'm hearing.

BABE. I think that's a perfectly fine explanation.

RUBY. Explanation, bullshit. You got something on your mind? You got some rumors you want to check out? You wanna say I torched my hock shop? Say it!

DONALD. You had a fire of unknown origins.

RUBY. You think it's easy running a business on the North Side these days? It's not like when you were on the barbecue circuit. I got guns behind every counter. Because they fuckin' hate me. Arson? Fuck you, arson. *(He throws down his cards.)*

DONALD. Number one, I don't give a shit if you torched your shop or not? Next riot it's toast anyway. Number two, I don't even see your smoke. On the news, now there's smoke. Watts, Southside Chicago, South Viet Nam. Hueys, 105s, napalm—we're talking serious smoke. A little girl with her clothes blown off and her skin melting like marshmallow. A Buddhist monk going like a fucking torch. And they want me to send my kid there? They want me to smoke my own flesh and blood? They got it once. That's all. No more. Number three, get over yourself. Your smoke, you can blow it out your ass for all I care about fencing goods and over-insuring a toilet of a building. I've seen smoke like you'll never know. And if I want to smoke the fucking queen from now until doomsday, I'll smoke the fucking queen!

(RUBY leaves. HERBIE follows. DONALD is eating everything within reach.)

BABE. You need help.

DONALD. I'm fine. Never felt better.

BABE. Whatever it is you're not talking about, you better talk about with somebody.

DONALD. Ruby just heard plenty. There's nothing more to talk about.

BABE. No? When's the last time either one of us slept through the night? You think you're going to fix it with food?

DONALD. Do me a favor, Babe. Go fuck yourself.

BABE. You'll never have another friend like me. *(Exits.)*

DONALD. For the record, he did torch his place and I don't give a fuck!

(DONALD cleans up. EV enters.)

EV. You can still catch Ruby before he gets in his car.

DONALD. Catch him? He's lucky I don't kill him.

EV. Over a misunderstanding? He thought you were criticizing how he handles his business.

DONALD. Business is booming. BOOM! Ruby's cleaning up on the insurance dough. BOOM, Babe is selling army fatigues to every hippie in town. BOOM, Purina just bought Herbie's yard to put up an office building, the guy's suddenly a real estate tycoon. BOOM, BOOM, BOOM! Anybody mention there's more to life than that? Anybody mention there's a fucking war on? *(He eats mechanically.)*

EV. What war is that?

DONALD. Not you, too? I'm the only sane one.

EV. Tell me what war? Stop feeding your face for one second and talk to me.

DONALD. You better get off my back with this fucking eating routine of yours.

EV. Don't you threaten me.

DONALD. Don't act like I'm some low-rent wife beater. Have I ever raised a hand to you?

EV. You raise your voice all the time. You throw words like punches. I'm black and blue with it, Donald. I can't live like this anymore.

DONALD. You want out of this marriage, just ask.

EV. I want to know why you are killing yourself with food.

DONALD. It's not me, it's them. They're killing me!

EV. What "them"?

DONALD *(deflated)*. The bank cut off my credit line.

EV. I don't understand. Explain that to me.

DONALD. The loan officer had all kinds of bullshit explanations. It's simple arithmetic—no credit no inventory, no inventory no sales. Any way you slice it, I'm finished.

EV. But you've got a working business. It doesn't make sense.

DONALD. It does if they're red-lining the neighborhood. My old man God-rest-his-soul was alive today, he'd go down there and strangle the bastards with his bare hands. Forget the fact that in twenty-five years Waldman Furniture never missed a single payment. Not even late. And they're putting me in Chapter 11!

EV. You'll find another bank.

DONALD. There is no other bank for that neighborhood. It's a done deal. I'm out of business. I went bust in a boom. How am I going to feed my family? Forgive me.

(EV reaches out to comfort him. He recoils and slumps into a recliner chair.)

And I sit. At least, she thinks I'm sitting. But I'm going molecular, melting, merging into the Naugahyde recliner. Senses shut down one by one like overloaded circuits. There goes touch, there goes smell, uh-oh, sight, taste! Leaving only the sounds in my head. Blood in the vein, pulsing, pounding. Distant thunder, coming closer, swallowing up all other sounds. Incoming. Boom. Boom. Boom.

First Light—Belgium (December 1944)

DONALD. First light. I'm like a man coming out of a cave. The sun glints off the snow. I look up and see strands of silver sparkling in the tall pines. Mike already has sunglasses on and he's telling me about how replacements are bad luck for vets. Mike is Mike Kourembanis, a large Greek out of Detroit who figured I wouldn't last the night in his foxhole.

Sounds to me like the replacements are having all the bad luck. I mean, whoever heard of a fucking foxhole before yesterday? It's trenches all over again. We might as well be fighting World War I.

MIKE. There's only one war, and it's been going on since the beginning of time. *(Chews a stick of gum.)*
DONALD. Are all Greeks philosophers?
MIKE. I'm the Greek who can show you how to stay alive. How's that for philosophy? Now gimme your wet socks.

(He places DONALD's socks over his shoulders to dry out in the sun.) That's how you dry 'em out so you don't get trench foot.

DONALD. What's that stuff in the trees?

MIKE. Tinsel.

DONALD. Is this how they celebrate Christmas over here?

MIKE. *Yamemene idiote!* You fucking idiot! Nobody's celebrating nothing. You heard our bomber group fly over last night? They drop tinsel to throw off the German radar. The shit's everywhere; in the trees, in your hair. Pick it outta your grub or you'll be shittin' it.

DONALD. It's kind of pretty.

MIKE. You're lucky it's only tinsel. Sometimes when the flak's too heavy our guys drop their bombs short of target and hightail it back to England. Guess who else is short of target? "Friendly fire." *(He takes the gum out of his mouth and grabs DONALD's dog tags.)*

DONALD. Hey, those're my dog tags.

MIKE. Yeah, well they sound like fucking Jingle Bells to a sniper. You gotta stick 'em together. *(He looks at the tags, rips them off his neck.)*

DONALD. Now whatta you doing?

MIKE. The Germans take prisoners, but not if you're wearing Jewish dog tags. *(Tosses them; a clanking sound.)* Holy shit!

DONALD. My dog tags bounce off a dud 88mm artillery shell up to its charge in snow. Close, huh?

MIKE. Tyheros Evreos.

DONALD. Mike decides I'm good luck. I've never been lucky in my life. You should see me play cards!

MIKE. You're my "lucky Jew," and that's that!

(A whistle blows.)

DONALD. The lieutenant moves us out through the pine forest. We're maybe one hundred yards away from the foxhole when... *(A huge explosion. They flatten out, then slowly rise.)* The dud explodes.

MIKE. Tyheros Evreos.

DONALD. Maybe I am lucky.

ECT (1968)

(DONALD tapes electrodes to his head.)

DONALD. I'm working on a new impression—"Frankenstein." The man leaning over me wears hospital white. I read the blue stitched lettering on the lab coat—"Barnes Hospital Department of Psychiatry."

PSYCHIATRIST *(a slight Germanic accent)*. Mr. Waldman, can you hear me? I remind you that electroconvulsive therapy is perfectly safe. The convulsions will pass. Meantime, you may experience some short-term memory loss. That is the path to deep memory which we must shock in order to rid you of depression.

DONALD. This is nothing. I'm a fighter.

PSYCHIATRIST. Don't resist, don't fight it. That way will be much easier. Ready? Again!

(Rising electric hum.)

DONALD. It's like a hot spike from ear to ear. Take it all. Only this moment. And the next. No more memory forever. *(The electric hum subsides.)* Three weeks in that fucking hospital, they finally let me have visitors. I mean, Ev's been coming from day one. Brought me there in my catatonic stupor, Christ's sake. Works a full day, gets the kids fed, comes every evening nothing-to-it like we were on vacation somewhere.

EV. How are you, sweetie?

DONALD. Ask Dr. Frankenstein.

EV. Dr. Honneger says you'll be out of here in no time.

DONALD. Notice anything weird about him?

EV. His accent's Swiss, not German.

DONALD. Not the accent.

EV. He's the most respected psychiatrist in St. Louis. He's treated bank presidents, senators...okay, he has a slight facial tic.

DONALD. Slight?

EV. It could be more of twitch.

DONALD. He's like Elvis on acid. He gets twitchier when he zaps me. My pain gives him pleasure.

EV. Don't talk crazy.

DONALD. Shhh! We're on a psychiatric ward. Can't use the "c" word. Is that what our friends are saying? "Donald finally lost his marbles."

EV. Not to me they're not. Listen, toots, there's something I've been wanting to say to you for a long while. How to say it? *(Beat.)* I met a man at Tune Town who swept me off my feet. A man who loves and laughs and eats and fights and fucks up BIG! A man whose heart is so full it's a wonder it doesn't burst. A man who would lay down his life for me. What I'm trying to say is I married the best slow dancer in the world. But even slow dancers stumble now and then. *(Kisses him and exits.)*

DONALD. God love her. God knows I do.

NURSE. Mr. Waldman, your three brothers from New Jersey are here to see you.

DONALD. I don't have any brothers.

NURSE *(offstage)*. I told them visits are limited to family members. I'll call security.

DONALD. Three...oh! my three brothers from Jersey. This short-term memory loss thing...show them in.

(BABE enters with RUBY and HERBIE, who holds a large shopping bag.)

BABE. So this is where you've been hiding.

DONALD. Anything to get away from the three of you and hearts.

HERBIE. St-st-st-st-stanley Sp-sp-spiegelman has been s-sitting in for you. *(He deals cards.)*

RUBY. You gotta come back. Herbie almost has a stroke every time he says his name.

HERBIE. F-fuck you.

DONALD. Look, Ruby, there's a lot of uh fragments bouncing around my head. And one of them...I might've said some things about your business...

RUBY. We were all under a lotta stress. Forget it. Somebody gonna lead?

(HERBIE leads.)

BABE. You lose some weight, Donnie?

DONALD. I don't have much of an appetite. Big news, "Donald Misses a Meal!" Besides, the medication they got me on, I don't know, I'm supposed to watch what I eat.

HERBIE. W-w-w-watch this!

(HERBIE empties the shopping bag—a kosher salami, bagels, a bag of Snickers. DONNIE inhales a Snickers.)

DONALD. Ahhhh.
BABE. This isn't gonna go bad with your medicine?

(DONALD chokes, sinks to the floor.)

HERBIE. He's f-f-fine.
BABE. Let's try diamonds.
DONALD. First lead oughta be safe. Ace.

(RUBY hesitates.)

HERBIE. T-tonight, huh?
RUBY. I'm thinking.
BABE. What's there to think ab—oh no.

(They all know RUBY has the queen.)

DONALD. You got a card to play, play it. I'm not a charity case. Play your hand!
RUBY. What's this make you think of? *(He displays the queen of spades.)*
DONALD. My hands around your throat!
RUBY. That's our Donnie! *(RUBY kisses him on the lips.)*
DONALD. We all have a good laugh. The nurses come in to confiscate the goodies and end up having a salami and Snickers party with us. I walk the guys down the hall and say good night. It takes me a half hour to find my

room again. Sure, the patients' charts are posted on the doors. I just can't remember my name.

The Forward Observer—How I Got the Luger (February 1945)

CAPT. SHWINKY *(offstage).* Waldman, front and center.

DONALD. The 71st Division has been attached to Patton's 3rd Army. We know this because we lost our CO in some strafing. And the guy they send over to "HQ" Battery is one of those spit and polish types the old bastard is so fond of.

(SHWINKY enters.)

CAPT. SHWINKY. Captain Vernon F. Shwinky.

DONALD. The proud pedigreed product of West Point and he's totally disgusted by the immigrant sons disgracing his country's uniform. Mike swears the "F" is for "fuckhead." I'm just wondering what's the difference between this home-grown Aryan and the Aryans we're chasing to the Siegfried Line.

CAPT. SHWINKY. You think you're a pretty tough hombre, soldier?

DONALD. I'm alive, sir.

CAPT. SHWINKY. Don't interrupt a superior, boy. You think you're tough 'cause you arm-wrestled some faggot stateside. That dog don't hunt, mister. You ain't tough six-oh-eight till you eat some shrapnel, till you get close enough to Jerry to smell his farts and tell me what he had for breakfast.

DONALD. First Reineck, now this. There has to be a redneck manual somewhere. Nobody could come up with this stuff on their own.

CAPT. SHWINKY. I'm gonna give you a chance to show me how tough you are. I'm puttin' you with the FO team headin' up river to Liege. We got us some Germans dug in on that railroad embankment and I want you to call in bull's-eyes, son.

DONALD. Yessir. I'm one tough hombre, Captain. You won't be disappointed. By the way, sir, those captain's bars you're wearing make one hell of a target.

(SHWINKY removes his bars and exits.)

"FO" for the uninitiated is military shorthand for Forward Observer. See, our troops are here. Their troops are there, dug in. Somebody's got to radio in enemy positions to our 105 howitzer batteries, which have to build off the first round. What's wrong with this picture? The Germans start firing at our FO crew. Our boys fire back. We get it coming and going. *(Shells shriek and explode.)* I dive for cover in a graveyard.

CAPT. SHWINKY *(offstage)*. Radio enemy coordinates, and that means now!

DONALD *(into a walkie-talkie)*. We've got a full company of the SS Norde Division on that embankment! Range two hundred yards. Fire for effect!

Captain Shwinky lays the first round thirty yards from our position. *(Into the walkie-talkie.)* You're right on our heads, asshole. Gimme a round sixty yards long, thirty yards right! *(Boom.)* That's the range. Gimme another round forty yards left! *(Boom.)*

Bulls-eye. Fire at will! 105s scream down like thunderbolts. Forty minutes of shelling and the elite SS Norde behaves like any other troops getting the shit kicked out of them—they run. *(Shelling continues in the distance.)* Mike and I move up with our infantry and there on the railroad embankment is an SS captain. *(He aims his rifle at the SS CAPTAIN. Rapidly, overlapping.)* Halt!

MIKE. *Hande hoch!* [Hands up!]

(The CAPTAIN's hand is gun-belt high.)

DONALD. *Nein! Nein!*
MIKE. *An der Kopf!* [On the head!]

(The CAPTAIN puts his hands on his head.)

DONALD. *Ich bin ein*, Waldman!
MIKE. I don't think you got the grammar right.
DONALD. What?
MIKE. I don't know, the verb, the noun...it ain't good German.
DONALD. Shut up and cover him while I get that Luger. Maybe you'd like me to speak to him in Yiddish. *(He takes the Luger from the holster.)*
SS CAPTAIN. Kike!

(He spits in DONALD's face. DONALD reflexively fires the Luger. The SS CAPTAIN falls. SHWINKY enters.)

CAPT. SHWINKY. Waldman!

DONALD. Sir?

CAPT. SHWINKY. KIA?

MIKE. You got that right, sir—killed in action, absolutely.

CAPT. SHWINKY. That's what he gets for wearing his captain's bars. Heavy casualties. Kourembanis, you're the new radio man. Waldman, you're unit leader. We'll get you your stripes later. *(He exits.)*

DONALD. Sergeant Donald L. Waldman. *Ich bin ein* Jew!

Precious Metal and Others (1977)

DONALD. I must really be slipping. I bought the *World Book Encyclopedia* from a wet-behind-the-ears salesman who couldn't sell breath to a dying man. I already slammed the door in his face when he shouted back...

SALESMAN. Studies have shown that if you read the *World Book* from A to Z, it's like having a college education.

DONALD. A throwaway line like that, but it stops me cold. Because when you eat like I eat, you're looking at some serious time on the toilet. And this can transform an average bathroom into a college classroom! *(To the SALESMAN.)* "Cost," less ten percent. *(Beat.)*

The bathroom is now known as "the library." Here's some of what I learned—the climate of coastal New Guinea is ideal for growing kumquats. The world began with a bang. Brass is an alloy of iron and copper that dates back to ancient Mesopotamia. What I most learned is that if you sit on a toilet that much, you're going to get the worst case of hemorrhoids in medical history. Has any man ever paid such a price for knowledge?

My youngest son is home from college. Being an authentic college boy, he knows everything about everything, even if he never read the *World Book*, cover to cover. He's taken the semester off to work on an Indian reservation, of all things...

SON. Not "Indian," Dad. That's the word of the oppressor. We call them Native Americans.
DONALD. Native sounds kinda oppressive to me. Tarzan stuff.
SON. Don't pick a fight. You're in over your head.
DONALD. Okay, Mr. Smart Guy. "America" comes from Amerigo Vespucci, who discovered South America and was just as Italian and imperialistic as Columbus, besides which, the Vikings beat them both by a few centuries, so why don't we call them Native Scandinavians or the Yohnsons?
SON. What makes you such an expert?
DONALD. The *World Book Encyclopedia*, is what!
SON. That makes you an expert on hemorrhoids. The point is, the Navajos are a third-world country right within our borders. And instead of trying to assimilate and obliterate their culture, we should help them preserve it.
DONALD. Preserve what, for instance?
SON. The concept of holism. The idea that true health is a balance of physical and spiritual well-being.
DONALD. I get that. My body is a temple.
SON. The way you eat, your body's going to be a small town.
DONALD. Okay, smart-ass, give me an example of holism.
SON. For starters, there's the "sweat lodge." They sit in unbearable steam heat, praying.

DONALD. I'd be praying for somebody to open a window. Anyway, that's a *shvitz!*

SON. A what?

DONALD. Running off to study another culture you don't even know your own. A *shvitz* is a Jewish sweat lodge!

So I drag him kicking and screaming to the JCC.

(They join BABE and RUBY in towels.)

SON. Wow! This is intense.

DONALD. What? You expected accountants, dentists? These are tough Jews. Sweating and complaining. Except for Herbie. He's out *shtupping*, as usual.

RUBY. What I wouldn't give to be a college kid nowadays. The broads. Bra-less. Jesus!

DONALD. How's that for an application essay?

SON. What's wrong, Ruby—you don't like business, anymore?

RUBY. Business? Business is lousy!

DONALD. What business? You're retired.

RUBY. Retirement is lousy.

BABE. I count the days. I just hope it comes while I can still pee a straight line.

DONALD. Speaking of peeing...

RUBY/BABE. Here we go.

DONALD. I remember when I was still on the road, I'm in Chicago to call on a new customer. I got just enough time to go to the john before a meeting. I look over at the next urinal and there is Lew Gerber.

RUBY. "*Kush mir un toches.*"

SON. What?

BABE. It means "kiss my ass." Kind of Lew's motto.

DONALD. Can I finish the fucking story? Anyway, so the normal thing to say is, "Hey, hi, Lew, long time no see." What I do is lean over that invisible line that separates one urinal from another, take a good look, and whisper, "Small world." Now I turn to Lew for the priceless reaction... and it's not Lew. Complete and total stranger. No use explaining. Christ, I'm never going to see the guy again, anyway. I run to the meeting and who's sitting across the desk from me?

ALL. The guy who isn't Lew Gerber.

DONALD. Small world.

BABE. You know Lew fell over with a heart attack last week?

RUBY. What're you talking about? I just saw him at the Chinese restaurant.

BABE. He ate at the Chinese restaurant and fell over dead.

DONALD. What did he order? *(A beat, then raucous laughter.)*

My son is viewing all of this with something between anthropological detachment and utter horror. We leave the steam room, we shower. It's a while since the two of us were in the altogether together. And the only thing he can think to ask is...

SON. What's that? That thing on your hip.

DONALD. Nothing. A scar.

SON. I can see that. What's it from?

DONALD. How should I know? The war, I guess.

SON. You guess. What is this passive-aggressive bullshit? You're always bringing up the war, but the minute I ask you anything in detail...

DONALD. A mine, okay?

SON. You stepped on a land mine?

DONALD. If I stepped on a bouncing Betty, buddy boy, you and I would not be having this conversation, because at the very least my testicles would not be here and, hence, neither would you.

SON. Details, remember? Details.

DONALD. Patrol. Reconnaissance. I was walking point. The guy trips a wire. They couldn't even find all his body parts. It was probably some shrapnel caught me.

SON. How come you never showed me the Purple Heart?

DONALD. I don't have one. Number one, you take a Purple Heart they send a letter home to your family. I'm gonna upset my mom because I'm too stupid to get out of the way? Number two, I'm still here. The poor bastard hit the wire was maybe your age. And I should accept a fucking medal?

SON. You know, I just read in the paper how the family of a GI requested his medals posthumously. That means...

DONALD. It means, "We know you're dead, but something came up."

SON. It's a legacy. A way of saying this is what I did in the war.

DONALD. You want to know what I really did in the war? I'll tell you what—none of your fucking business!

SON. None of my fucking business? Was it my fucking business when you punched out my Little League coach for benching me? Was it my fucking business when you got arrested for mooning Nixon's motorcade? Was it my fucking business when you went into that hospital and I didn't know if you were ever coming out again? You are my fucking business. And I'm yours. Deal with it. *(Exits.)*

DONALD. The mouth on that kid. I don't know where he gets it. But he has a point. So I draft a letter to Army Central Records: "To whom it may concern: I'm still alive, but something just came up..."

ARMY RECORDS OFFICIAL. "Dear Mr. Waldman: After reviewing your request, we regret to inform you that there is no record of you ever having served in the Armed Forces of the United States."

DONALD. That's the army I remember. No record? Fuck you, no record. Now I'm pissed, and I send letters to my congressman, my senator, the president, himself. Two months later, I get a box stamped "Official." *(He opens the box.)* Medals all over the place. Medals I didn't ask for, didn't want. Bronze Star, Silver Star, and at the bottom of the pile, a Purple Heart. I call my son and calmly explain, "If you don't come over here and get these fucking things today, I'm flushing them down the toilet!"

(The SON enters, grabs the box, finds a hidden Snickers bar.)

DONALD. How did that get there?

SON. Why hide it? Eat it, go ahead. I'll buy you some more. A box, a case. So what if your heart is hitting on three cylinders? Go for it, eat yourself to death. Come to think of it, you're an impatient man, why wait? Why not take a bite out of the big enchilada?

DONALD. And he's reaching through the sweaters and sweatshirts in my closet and into the coffee can on the top shelf. The perfect hiding place that nobody could find in a million years...the Luger. *(To SON.)* How the hell did you know about that?

SON. Since I was five. The minute you and mom went out. I imagined the stories that went with it. Imagined what you must've gone through. Imagined I was you. It's loaded. With bullets, not food. What'll it be? You wanna throw something down the toilet, throw that. *(He slams the Purple Heart down, exits.)*

DONALD. I look at the Luger. I smell the gun oil. I see the lightning bolt insignia on the uniform collar. I feel the spit on my face. I eat the Snickers in one bite.

Mike's Luck (April 1945)

VOICE 1. Anybody from 6th Armored?

DONALD. Since we crossed the Siegfried Line, the mechanized elements of the 2nd Squadron are moving so fast the SS doesn't have time to remove their prisoners.

VOICE 2. Anybody from 71st Engineers?

DONALD. We're liberating one POW camp after another. I'm talking a sea of smiles.

VOICE 3. Anybody from Dallas?

DONALD. These liberators are walking into the camps figuring they might find somebody from their unit, even from back home.

VOICE 4. Anybody from South Philly?

DONALD. So we're at Waldensburg in the Rhineland. There's gotta be 6500 Allied prisoners...

BROOKLYN VOICE 1. Anybody from Flatbush?

DONALD. Flatbush! What're the odds? Stupid, right?

BROOKLYN VOICE 2. Avenue U and Ralph!

BROOKLYN VOICES. Fuckin' guy! Get outta here!

DONALD. "Anybody from St. Louis?" And this nasal little voice calls back...

BROOKLYN SOLDIER. "*Kush mir un toches?*" *(Exits.)*
DONALD. Lew Gerber! Small world!

(He and MIKE are walking patrol.)

MIKE. Where was I?
DONALD. How should I know? It was total chaos.
MIKE. Waldensburg was last week. How come you're only telling me now?
DONALD. I didn't think you'd appreciate it.

Mike mopes. But I barely notice because it's one of those bright April days, you know, the kind that breaks your heart. When you just spent an entire winter out of doors, any warmth is heartbreaking.

The "HQ" battery FO unit is on foot with the front-line infantry rooting out German stragglers from a birch forest outside Ohrdorf. One of those Brooklyn guys remembers it's Passover and says we oughta do a Seder. I spot a farmhouse in a rolling meadow beyond the tree line. It's bound to have some eggs, maybe even some wine. I bet that cow grazing at the side of the barn might even be persuaded to donate a brisket. So when Captain Shwinky says...

CAPT. SHWINKY. I need two volunteers to reconnoiter that location.
DONALD/MIKE. Yessir!
CAPT. SHWINKY. Keep your spacing, soldiers! This ain't a cakewalk. This is enemy territory.
MIKE *(mutters)*. Kiss my ass.

DONALD. That at me or Shwinky?

MIKE. "*Kush mir un toches*" means "kiss my ass." You coulda told me the story.

DONALD. Who knew you speak Yiddish?

MIKE. German. Back in Detroit, the gang in the next neighborhood was German. You have a German name.

DONALD. Yeah, well before they ran us outta Russia, they ran us outta Germany. Honest to Christ, I didn't know which army to join.

MIKE. It means "forest," in case you're interested. "Woods."

DONALD. My name means Woodsman? I like that.

MIKE. Or maybe it means you can't see the forest for the trees.

DONALD. You going philosophical on me again?

MIKE. I know what's eatin' you. Believe me, situation was reversed that Kraut bastard would've killed you for laughs.

DONALD. Then what's him and what's me?

MIKE. Him is he thinks you got less right to live than that cow out there.

DONALD. And me?

MIKE. You is he fucked with the wrong Jew! *(MIKE pauses to light a smoke. The flint is gone on his lighter.)* Damned lighter.

DONALD. I'm digging in my field jacket for my Zippo when ... *(The crack of a rifle.)* I see the white puff from the farmhouse. *(He flattens. MIKE is on his knees.)* He could've been praying, except for the confused look on his face. The stupid look. *(He fires back, emptying his clip, then takes MIKE in a fireman's carry.)* I glance back, the fucking cow doesn't even flinch. The Brooklyn guy runs out to help us and trips a bouncing Betty. *(Ex-*

plosion! DONALD is knocked off his feet. He's wounded in the hip, but all he can think about is MIKE.) Medic!
CAPT. SHWINKY. He's gone, boy. Get a grip on yourself.
DONALD. Medic!!!
CAPT. SHWINKY. I'm gonna recommend you for the Silver Star.
DONALD. You do, and I'll kill you!

Before Shwinky can open his mouth to say "court-martial," the retrieval team drags the sniper over for everyone to get a good look. I hit him enough times, there's not much to look at. A kid.

CAPT. SHWINKY. This is your lucky day, boy. It's Passover and the Angel of Death just flew right by you. I want you to scout out some high ground outside Weimar for "A" and "B" batteries. Now get the hell out of my sight.
DONALD. I look back at Mike. He's gone small, like you do when the last breath is out of you. When your lucky Jew lets you down.

I find a driver and grab a jeep with a .50 mounted on the back. We take off down a logging road through the Thurgin Forest and come out on a high plain overlooking one mother of a POW camp. The driver radios back to company.

DRIVER. The CO says to wait for reinforcements.
DONALD. Fuck that. Let's have a look.

When In Rome (1989)

DONALD. Ev and I have been wanting to get away since before I can remember. I opened a new store and it's actually going like crazy. Strictly high-end, special order. Thirty-five days to your door, or your money back. And selection? You name it, we've got it. Any fabric under the sun, except Naugahyde. I got a thing about it. I'd close up and go back on the road before Naugahyde. It's an anniversary present, the trip. I tell Ev we can go anywhere she wants. I'm thinking Miami Beach, L.A., Vegas, she comes up with...

EV. Rome.

DONALD. Why Rome?

EV. It's different.

DONALD. I'll tell you what's different about Rome—it's in Italy. And in case you didn't pick up a newspaper before 1945, Italy was on *their* side!

EV. We have three children and they drive a Volkswagen, a Toyota and a Fiat. In case you haven't picked up a paper since 1945, the war is over. Maybe it's time you stopped fighting it.

DONALD. I'm not fighting anything and I'm not going to Rome. End of discussion!

So here we are in Rome. She shops, I eat. Strange thing about eating in Italy, no matter how much and how fast you eat—you taste it. Pasta fazule, calamari, scungilli, another mouthful I swear I'll burst into Puccini. So we're walking it off. Right. What I ate for lunch, alone, I'd have to walk to China. Ev is wearing the brand new pair of $300 Gucci pumps that look unbelievable, even if they don't feel all that great. She's massaging the blister on her big toe and I'm thinking some tira misu might get me to the next meal, when I notice a star. In this city of all cities, the Pope's backyard—a synagogue!

We're inside two seconds and a woman shuffles over, my age at least.

ROSE *(Italian accent)*. GI?
DONALD. I haven't heard that in years. Donald.
ROSE. Rosa. *(They shake hands.)* Me and my husband lived outside Rome before the war. Ran a little tailor shop. "Shmatas."
DONALD. Fine hand-sewn garments, I bet.
ROSE. *Como se dici*—it was a living. The Fascisti didn't give up their Jews. But the Nazis came in toward the end of the war, the deportations started. We were sent to separate camps. May God remember! I love the GIs. The GIs liberated my camp.
DONALD. Your husband loves the GIs, too?
ROSE. Even more, they tell me. But he died on liberation day at Buchenwald.
DONALD. I can't speak.
ROSE. *Shalom*. Peace. Please. Peace.
DONALD. And I'm outside, bent over a trash bin.
EV. What is it, Donald?
DONALD. Something I ate.

It Is Revealed (April 11, 1945)

DONALD. I drive down a logging road through the Thurgin Forest and come out at one mother of a POW camp.

The guard towers are empty. Not a single sentry. The electrified gate is wide open. The driver wants to stay back with the jeep. "Maybe it's already liberated."

But I know better. What tells me? The smell. Good God, the smell. I know it from the battlefield, the bodies rotting in the April sun. There are no words to describe it. If there are POWs here, they are past liberating. I lower my rifle and walk. Out of nowhere, they start appearing. Not army green. Stripes.

PRISONERS. GI, GI, GI...

DONALD. First a few, then a dozen, then hundreds.

PRISONERS. GI, GI, GI...

DONALD. I'm pulling K-rations from my pack. All gone in an instant. Still, they keep coming.

PRISONERS. GI, GI, GI!...

DONALD. What are you? What have you become? How could you let them turn you into animals, more dead than alive? The stink of death is on you. How do I liberate the dead? Shame on you. Shame! *(The voices stop.)*

I fall between the ticks of a clock. I wander, the Forward Observer, wordless among worn, yellow stars and windowless barracks as silent as coffins. I blink back tears and my eyelids are like shutters, snapping incomprehensible pictures: a bloodstained meat hook double-bolted into a reinforced concrete wall; a cast-iron furnace door still hot to the touch; an infinite knot of naked limbs; a windblown spiral of ash. Passover rewritten, undone.

I'm standing outside Barracks #39. A man staggers towards me, a half-eaten K-ration in his hand.

PRISONER. *Veist oys.* It is revealed.
DONALD. Nothing is revealed. You don't even know who I am!
PRISONER. *Veist oys.*
DONALD. That you let them reduce you to this just to survive. I'm a fighter, a warrior!
PRISONER. *Veist oys.*
DONALD. How could you do this to yourself?
PRISONER. *Veist oys.*
DONALD. I'm one of you. I'm you. How could you do this to me?! He sinks to the ground. The air hisses out of him like a leaking balloon, and he dies. I look to my left, to my right—they are dying all around me.

Why are you dying? You've been liberated. I risked everything to be here. Lost my way. Lost my best friend. Lost myself. Lost...to find you...to save you. I have come to Buchenwald! And you won't even save yourselves? Why are you dying? Why?

Got vet shtrofen! God will punish!

Hearts #3—Further Lessons In Eating (The Present)

(DONALD holds the "M" volume of the World Book.*)*

DONALD. Malnutrition is the organism's response to extreme deprivation. For lack of food, the body begins to... Let me put it another way. There's a cannibal inside every one of us. Not something with a necklace of shrunken skulls and a spear. More like a switch. The Cannibal Switch. When you stop feeding your body, your stomach says, "Okay, I'll find my own food." Click, before you know it, you're eating like a king. Only catch is, you're eating yourself alive. And along comes an actual meal. Maybe it's only K-rations. But it packs the protein wallop of porterhouse. Now the stomach is baffled. It has forgotten how to eat real food. How to be human. So it turns to the heart. And the heart, empty, cannibalized, heartsick...stops. Just shuts down the whole works. Hearts don't forget what it is to be human.

(DONALD puts away the volume and plays hearts with BABE and HERBIE. HERBIE offers some candy but DONALD declines.)

HERBIE. Th-th-this some new kinda diet, D-don?
DONALD. Sure, a diet. *(Throws in the cards.)* Three-handed sucks.
HERBIE. You g-g-got a b-better idea?
DONALD. Three into fifty-two does not go. There's an odd card.
BABE. That's why we put it face down in the first trick.
DONALD. It could be anything—a picture, a heart...
HERBIE. Th-the queen?
DONALD. Only when I take the trick.
BABE. You don't like three-handed, you should've told Ruby not to drop dead from a coronary.
HERBIE. E-e-e-e-easy f-f-or you t-to say.

*(After a long silence they burst out laughing; they laugh till they cry, then go on laughing through tears—*lachen mit yash-tsherkes.*)*

BABE. You find a fourth, let me know.
HERBIE *(with an effort, stutterless)*. Next week?
DONALD. Next week.

(HERBIE exits.)

BABE. I was thinking about how you wrote away for your medals.
DONALD. It was my kid's idea. Dumbest thing I ever did. Threw them away.
BABE. No you didn't.
DONALD. Every last one, down the toilet.
BABE. If you say so. Donnie, there is no next week.
DONALD. Hey, no tumors, no neurological anatomical urological this or that. I do not give you permission to die on me.
BABE. Nobody's dying. Nancy and I are moving to Florida.
DONALD. Even worse!
BABE. They've got golf, corned beef. How bad can it be?
DONALD. How about hurricanes? How about three hundred percent humidity? How about summer alone will kill you?
BABE. Summer I'll spend here.
DONALD. The hell you will.
BABE. The hell I will. You know, a funny thing happened when I put down the deposit on the condo. That night, I slept like a baby. God forgave me. Closed my eyes at ten-fifteen and didn't open them again until eight

o'clock the next morning. Didn't wake up once. Not to pee. Not to dance. Not to wonder why fifty years ago in Germany I... *(Beat.)* I never told you why I don't sleep.

DONALD. I never told you why I eat.

BABE. I know.

DONALD. I know.

BABE *(embraces DONALD)*. Give yourself a break sometime, huh?

DONALD. I'm working on it.

BABE. So, you gonna play gin with Herbie?

DONALD. Number one, I'd cut off my hands first.

BABE. And number two? For once, you forgot number two.

DONALD. Fuck you.

BABE. I love you, too.

The Forward Observer Lost In Cyberspace
(The Present, and a Day)

DONALD. My kids gave me a computer for my retirement. This for a guy who needs directions to screw in a light bulb. They tell me you can play cards, but the opponents have names like Michelle and Bruce and Chip. You can't play cards with people like that. Even cyber people.

Then my granddaughter tells me about e-mail. What's wrong with envelopes and stamps? What do I need with that?

GRANDDAUGHTER. It's instant. And you can send dirty jokes... instantly.

DONALD. Bingo! Babe and I are e-mailing all day long. It's not bad, but it's not like a real kibitz. That's when my grandkid tells me about "chat" rooms. I don't chat in person. Why should I do it through a bunch of wires?

GRANDDAUGHTER. But, Poppy, if you're not chatting online, you're nowhere.

DONALD. Even if you are nowhere, you don't want your grandkid to know it. So she presses a few buttons, and before I know it, I'm in something called a "senior chat room."

What do I have to chat about with complete strangers who are probably senile and wearing diapers?

GRANDDAUGHTER. You never know, Poppy, sometimes you bump into people you kinda know but didn't realize it.

DONALD. I can do that looking into a mirror.

GRANDDAUGHTER. Don't be so local. You gotta be global.

DONALD. I've been global. I'll take local.

GRANDDAUGHTER. I'm putting you in the chat room, and that's that.

DONALD. And she does. What she doesn't mention is that one room leads to the next. From my "senior" chat room, I graduate to a "senior Jewish chat room," which they might as well call a senior Jewish "*kvetch*" room. Here, let me show you.

(Projection of monitor screen.)

Log on: THE SENIOR JEWISH EATING-DISORDER CHAT ROOM.

This one has no appetite, that one has no end of appetite. I mention my tendency to overeat. "When did this problem begin?" "You want an exact date? Some time after the war." "Have you ever been treated for post traumatic stress disorder?"

(Projection.)

Log on: THE SENIOR JEWISH COMBAT VETERANS CHAT ROOM.

But nobody's chatting. People are confessing. People are spilling their guts about war-induced pain and depression and alcoholism and insomnia and overeating and depth therapy, group therapy, shock therapy...and it's merely a short hop to...

(Projection.)

Log on: THE HOLOCAUST SURVIVORS CHAT ROOM.

Survivor. Whose word is that? Is that all they are? Is that all I am? I was a soldier, a warrior! I fought, I killed...I...

(He types almost automatically; projection.)

"On April 11th, 1945, I entered Buchenwald sector B as a forward observer with the 71st Infantry Division of the American 3rd Army. And outside barracks #39, I killed people with food."

If God is in the wires, why doesn't he strike me dead? I'm waiting! What's the matter—no guts? I don't even sign off. I turn off the computer. Pull the plug. Days go by, weeks. My granddaughter calls on the telephone, and right away she's busting my balls.

GRANDDAUGHTER. Why aren't you answering your e-mail?
DONALD. Something's wrong with the computer.
GRANDDAUGHTER. Nothing's wrong with the computer. Gramma told me.
DONALD. Gramma knows so much, why can't she keep the time from flashing on the VCR?
GRANDDAUGHTER. She told me you pulled the plug two weeks ago. That's rude. That's like leaving the phone off the hook. Like locking the mailbox shut.
DONALD. They're going next. From now on I can only be reached by personal audience.
GRANDDAUGHTER. That's worse than rude—that's chickenshit.
DONALD. Who are you to call me chickenshit?
GRANDDAUGHTER. I'm my grandfather's granddaughter.
DONALD. Insults will get you nowhere.
GRANDDAUGHTER. Turn it on! Turn on the goddamn computer or I'm coming over and turning it on myself. I mean it! Bye, Poppy.
DONALD. Who could say "no" to that?

(Click. Projection.)

AOL VOICE. "WELCOME. YOU'VE GOT MAIL."

Mail. Six jokes from Babe, one so old we were telling it to each other in the tenth grade. And an offer to see

Jamie Lee Curtis with her shirt off. That's two weeks of e-mail?

But there's something else. An "attachment." I never had one of these. My grandkid said never download attachments from an unknown source—it could contain a virus. At my age, it's the virus that better be worried. I download the file and it's from Israel, of all places. Tel Aviv. What now, naked pictures of Golda Meir?

It's a photo of a man named Sam Moultan. "Shmuel." He read my cyber-confession and wonders where I went to.

(More projections.)

My computer broke.

SHMUEL. I'm glad to see it's fixed. I hope some computer geek goniff didn't take you for a bundle.
DONALD. I like this guy already.

The only gonif I know is the phone company. All this e-mailing is making somebody a fortune.

SHMUEL. You're telling me. But what can I do? The computer was my granddaughter's idea.
DONALD. A universal truth!
SHMUEL. Ready for another one? I read what you wrote—that you killed people with food. No GI killed a single prisoner in a concentration camp. The effects of extreme malnutrition are often irreversible. The Nazis had set the mechanism of death in motion long before

you arrived. You came and offered food. You offered love.

DONALD. If you're trying to grant absolution, you're way out of your league.

SHMUEL. I'll tell you about my "league." On April 11th, 1945, I was in barracks #39 at Buchenwald. I weighed sixty pounds. I was too weak to walk out to greet my liberators. But I could see you through a crack in the wall planks. I remember a slender man with dark hair, sergeant's stripes, and a kind face drenched with tears.

DONALD. That could have been anybody.

SHMUEL. A man stood before you and said, "*Veist oys*. It is revealed." Was that you he said it to?

DONALD *(beat)*. The hair is thin and gray. And if you could see me, slender is not the first word that would come to mind. But the rest is me. Yes, that was me. I wonder to this day, what did he mean? What was "revealed"?

SHMUEL. That we are survivors.

DONALD. Not survivors. Warriors!

SHMUEL. Yes, that is the better word—warriors.

DONALD. But nothing is revealed.

SHMUEL. We are revealed to each other across oceans, across space, across time, across heartbeats. Now that we found each other, may we stay in touch?

DONALD. By phone? The bills will be astronomical.

SHMUEL. You never heard of "collect"?

DONALD. Now that's a revelation! We are in touch. We... touch.

SHMUEL. *Shalom.*

DONALD. *Shalom.* Peace.

I sign off. I leave the computer on. I find the hum of it somehow comforting. Not white noise. Not the absence of sound. But an inspiriting presence. Every voice ever spoken since the first day of Creation. Filled with life and nurture like a womb, or a prayer in the ear of God. It washes over me.

EV *(offstage)*. Donald?
DONALD. Her voice is like music.
EV *(enters)*. You're not eating in here, are you?
DONALD. Me? Eating? I'm just straightening out a few things.

(He lovingly picks up the Ike jacket from the floor and drapes it over the back of the computer chair. He switches on a CD player. Jo Stafford sings "I'll Be Seeing You." EV starts to leave, but DONALD reaches out with his hand. She takes it and they slow dance. For a moment, they are romantic, ageless.)

EV *(sexy)*. Dinner's ready. *(She exits.)*

(He opens a drawer and removes a blue velvet jewelry case from which he takes the Purple Heart. He dangles it from one finger so it catches the otherworldly blue light from the computer screen. He pins the heart to the jacket, and exits.)

THE END

DIRECTOR'S NOTES

DIRECTOR'S NOTES

DIRECTOR'S NOTES

DIRECTOR'S NOTES